THE

COMPLETE

USER GUIDE

TO

APPLE WATCH 4

This document is geared towards providing exact and reliable information in regards to the topic and issue covered. The publication is sold with the idea that the publisher is not required to render accounting, officially permitted, or otherwise, qualified services. If advice is necessary, legal or professional, a practiced individual in the profession should be ordered.

- From a Declaration of Principles which was accepted and approved equally by a Committee of the American Bar Association and a Committee of Publishers and Associations.

In no way is it legal to reproduce, duplicate, or transmit any part of this document in either electronic means or in printed format. Recording of this publication is strictly prohibited and any storage of this document is not allowed unless with written permission from the publisher. All rights reserved.

The information provided herein is stated to be truthful and consistent, in that any liability, in terms of inattention or otherwise, by any usage or abuse of any policies, processes, or directions contained within is the solitary and utter responsibility of the recipient reader. Under no circumstances will any legal responsibility or blame be held against the publisher for any reparation, damages, or monetary loss due to the information herein, either directly or indirectly.

Respective authors own all copyrights not held by the publisher.

The information herein is offered for informational purposes solely, and is universal as so. The presentation of the information is without contract or any type of guarantee assurance.

The trademarks that are used are without any consent, and the publication of the trademark is without permission or backing by the trademark owner. All trademarks and brands within this book are for clarifying purposes only and are the owned by the owners themselves, not affiliated with this document.

Table of Contents

INTRODUCTION

When you take your Apple Watch out of the box, it's the same as everyone else's. What makes your smartwatch personal is the style and the apps, which mean your Apple Watch will be uni☐ue to your needs.

What does the Apple Watch do is one of the common ☐uestions among people looking to buy the Apple Watch for the first time?

Well, a lot more than just offering you the chance to read text messages and answer calls on your wrist, rather than your phone, which is the main feature everybody knows.

The Apple Watch is a competent fitness tracker, with some world class features, and can double as a sports watch too.

Yes, you can spend less time looking at your phone with wrist notifications, and thanks to having Siri on your wrist, setting alarm timers and reminders is simple, too.

Then there's dedicated apps. From boarding passes to traffic notifications and walking directions, it's a very personal experience.

The launch of Apple watch 4 also refreshed the features on offer too. Advanced heart rate metrics, new watch faces and an alarm that tells you if your heart is going wrong, the Apple Watch does a lot more than just calls and texts.

The Apple Watch has an undeniably steep learning curve, and the first 24 hours can be a little frustrating for the uninitiated. Check out this guide on how to use the Apple Watch, including all the new features and interface tweaks.

Let's get started

CHAPTER 1

USING MAP FOR DIRECTIONS
WITH APPLE WATCH

Apple Watch has a Maps glance for a quick look at your location and surroundings, and a full Maps app for exploring and getting directions. "Show Berlin on the map."

See a map. Open the Maps app on Apple Watch. Or, for a quick look at your location, swipe up on your watch face, then swipe to the Maps glance. Tap the Maps glance to open the full Maps app.

You are here.

Tap to center on your current location.

Pan and zoom. To pan the map, drag with one finger. To zoom in or out, turn the Digital Crown.

You can also double-tap the map to zoom in on the spot you tap. Tap the Tracking button in the lower left to get back to your current location.

Search the map. While viewing the map, firmly press the display, tap Search, then tap Dictate or tap a location in the list of places you've explored recently.

Get info about a landmark or location. Tap the location on the map, then turn the Digital

Crown to scroll the information. Tap < in the upper left to return to the map.

Stick a pin. Touch and hold the map where you want the pin to go, wait for the pin to drop, then let go.

Now you can tap the pin for address information, or use it as the starting point or destination for directions. To move the pin, just drop a new one in the new location.

Get address info or use as a starting point.

Find the approximate address of any spot on the map. Drop a pin on the location, then tap the pin to see address info.

Call a location. Tap the phone number in the location info. To switch to iPhone, swipe up on the Phone icon in the lower-left corner of the Lock screen, then tap the green bar at the top of the screen.

See a contact's address on the map. While viewing the map, firmly press the display, tap Contacts, turn the Digital Crown to scroll, then tap the contact.

See your current location and surroundings. Open Maps, then tap the current location arrow in the lower left.

Or swipe to the Maps glance, which always shows where you are. If you have an upcoming calendar event, the Maps glance shows directions to it.

Get directions

Get directions to a landmark or map pin. Open Maps, then tap the destination landmark or map pin. Scroll the location information until you see Directions, then tap Walking or Driving.

When you're ready to go, tap Start, then follow the directions.

Get directions to a search result or contact. While viewing the map, firmly press the display, then tap Search or Contacts.

Ask Siri for directions. Just tell Siri where you'd like to go. "Directions to the nearest gas station?"

Follow directions. After you tap Start and head off on your first leg, Apple Watch uses taps to let you know when to turn.

A steady series of 12 taps means turn right at the intersection you're approaching; three pairs of two taps means turn left. Not sure what your destination looks like?

You'll feel a vibration when you're on the last leg, and again when you arrive.

Check your progress. Swipe left on the current step of the directions, or tap the dots at the bottom of the screen to see a map view.

Estimated time of arrival

Firmly press to stop directions.

Find out when you'll get there. Look in the upper-left corner for your estimated time of arrival.

Current time is in the upper right.
End directions before you get there. Firmly press the display, then tap Stop Directions.

CHAPTER 2

PLAY MUSIC ON APPLE WATCH

You can store music right on Apple Watch, then listen to it on Bluetooth headphones or speakers without your iPhone nearby.

Store songs on Apple Watch. Open the Apple Watch app on iPhone, tap My Watch, go to Music > Synced Playlist, then choose the playlist of songs you want to move to Apple Watch.

Then, place Apple Watch on its charger to complete the sync. When the music has been synced, open the Settings app on Apple Watch, go to General >

About, and look under Songs to see the number of songs copied.

You can use the Music app on iPhone to create a playlist specifically for music you want to listen to on Apple Watch.

Pair Bluetooth headphones or speakers. Follow the instructions that came with the headphones or speakers to put them in discovery mode.

When the Bluetooth device is ready, open the Settings app on Apple Watch, tap Bluetooth, then tap the device when it appears.

Play songs stored on Apple Watch. Open Music on Apple Watch, firmly press the display, tap Source, then choose Watch.

Control playback. Swipe to the Now Playing glance for ☐uick control. Swipe up on the watch face, then swipe to the playback controls. You can also control playback using the Music app.

Limit the songs stored on Apple Watch. Open the Apple Watch app on iPhone, tap My Watch, go to Music > Playlist Limit, then choose a storage limit or maximum number of songs to be stored on Apple Watch.

See how much music is stored on Apple Watch. On Apple Watch, open the Settings app , go to General > About, and look under Songs.

CHAPTER 3

VIEW PHOTOS ON APPLE WATCH

Photos from the iPhone album of your choice are stored on Apple Watch, and appear in the Photos app on Apple Watch.

When you first get Apple Watch, it's set to use your Favorites album—photos you've tagged as favorite but you can change the album it uses.

Tap to view a photo.

Browse photos on Apple Watch. Open the Photos app on Apple Watch, then tap a photo.

Swipe left or right to see others. Turn the Digital Crown to zoom or drag to pan. Zoom all the way out to see the entire album.

• Turn to zoom.
• Drag to pan.
• Double-tap to fill screen or see all.
• Swipe left or right to see the next photo.
• Choose your album

Apple Watch stores photos from a single synced photo album on your iPhone.

Choose the album to store on Apple Watch. Open the Apple Watch app on iPhone, tap My Watch, go to Photos > Synced Album, then choose the album. To create a new album for Apple Watch photos, use the Photos app on iPhone.

Choose the album to include on Apple Watch.

The actual number of photos stored on Apple Watch depends on available storage.

Manage photo storage

To save space on Apple Watch for songs or other content, you can limit the number of photos stored on Apple Watch.

Limit photo storage. Open the Apple Watch app on iPhone, tap My Watch, then go to Photos > Photos Limit. Look below Photos Limit to see how much Apple Watch storage is currently used by photos.

Set the limit for photos on Apple Watch.

How many photos? To see how many photos are on Apple Watch, open Settings on Apple Watch, then go to General > About. Or, open the Apple Watch app on iPhone, tap My Watch, then go to General > About.

CHAPTER 4

STOCKS

Track stocks

Use the Stocks app on Apple Watch to see info on the stocks you follow on your iPhone.

"What was today's closing price for Apple stock?"

Follow the market. To browse your stocks, open the Stocks app on Apple Watch.

See details about a stock. Tap it in the list, then turn the Digital Crown to scroll. Tap the performance graph (or the time indicators below it) to change the time scale. Tap < in the upper left to return to the stocks list.

Turn the Digital Crown to see more details.

Add, delete, or reorder stocks. Add, delete, or change the order of stocks using the Stocks app on iPhone. Changes you make there are reflected on Apple Watch.

Choose the data you see. Open the Stocks app on iPhone, then tap the Points Change for any stock to see Percentage Change or Market Cap.

Switch to Stocks on iPhone. While looking at the Stocks app or Stocks glance on Apple Watch, swipe up on the Stocks icon in the lower-left corner of the iPhone Lock screen.

Check one stock at a glance

Use the Stocks glance to check one stock of particular interest.

View the Stocks glance. Swipe up on the watch face, then swipe to the stock info.

Tap the glance to open the Stock app.

If you don't see the Stocks glance, open the Apple Watch app on iPhone, then go to My Watch > Glances and add it to your list of glances.

Choose your stock. Open the Apple Watch app on iPhone, tap My Watch, tap Stocks, then choose your default stock.

Choose the stock shown in the Stocks glance.

Add stock info to your watch face

You can add stock info to these faces:

• Modular (ticker name and price)
• Utility (ticker name, price, and change)
• Mickey Mouse (ticker name, price, and change)

Add stock info to a watch face. While viewing the face, firmly press the display, then tap Customize. Swipe left until you can select individual face features, tap the one you'd like to use, then turn the Digital Crown to choose

Stocks. When you're finished, press the Digital Crown.

Choose the stock shown on the watch face. Open the Apple Watch app on iPhone, tap My Watch, tap Stocks, then choose a default stock. If you choose Mirror iPhone, the stock shown on the watch face is the last one you highlighted in the Stocks app on iPhone.

Choose the data you see on the watch face. Open the Apple Watch app on iPhone, tap My Watch, tap Stocks, then tap Current Price, Points Change, Percentage Change, or Market Cap.

CHAPTER 5

WEATHER

See weather on your watch face

You can include weather info on these watch faces:

• Utility (temperature, or temperature and conditions)

• Modular (temperature, or temperature, conditions, high, and low)

• Simple (temperature)

• Color (temperature)

• Chronograph (temperature)

• Mickey Mouse (temperature, or temperature and conditions)

Add weather to your watch face. While viewing the face, firmly press the display, then tap

Customize. Swipe left until you can select individual face features, tap the one where you'd like to see weather info, then turn the Digital Crown to choose Weather. When you're finished, press the Digital Crown.

Tap temperature to open the Weather app.

Choose the city for the watch face weather. Open the Apple Watch app on iPhone, tap My Watch, then go to Weather > Default City.

Open the full Weather app. Tap the temperature on the watch face.

Accessibility and Related Settings

The Accessibility Shortcut

You can set the Digital Crown to turn either VoiceOver or Zoom on or off with a triple-click.

Set the Accessibility Shortcut. Open the Apple Watch app on iPhone, tap My Watch, go to General > Accessibility > Accessibility Shortcut, then choose VoiceOver or Zoom.

Use the shortcut. Press the Digital Crown ☐uickly three times. Triple-click the Digital Crown again to turn off the accessibility feature.

CHAPTER 6

VOICEOVER

Climate models are computer operated simulation programs that give climatologists a way to predict climate changes due to the changes in natural concentration of greenhouse gases and alterations in earth's natural ecosystems and habitats.

VoiceOver helps you use Apple Watch even if you can't see the display. Use simple gestures to move around the screen and listen as VoiceOver speaks each item you select.

Turn on VoiceOver. On Apple Watch, open the Settings app, then turn on General > Accessibility > VoiceOver.

You can also use iPhone to turn on VoiceOver for Apple Watch—open the Apple Watch app on iPhone, tap My Watch, then tap the VoiceOver option in General >

Accessibility. Or, use the Accessibility Shortcut. And there's always Siri: "Turn VoiceOver on."

Explore the screen. Move your finger around on the display and listen as the name of each item you touch is spoken.

You can also tap with one finger to select an item, or swipe left or right with one finger to select an adjacent item.

Swipe left or right, up or down with two fingers to see other pages. (For example, swipe up with two fingers on the watch face to see glances, then swipe left or right with two fingers to see the different glances.)

Go back. Gone down a path you didn't expect? Do a two-finger scrub: use two fingers to trace a "z" shape on the display.

Act on an item. With VoiceOver on, use a double tap instead of a single tap to open an app, switch an option, or perform any action that would normally be done with a tap.

Select an app icon or option switch by tapping it or swiping to it, then double-tap to perform its action.

For example, to turn VoiceOver off, select the VoiceOver button, then double-tap anywhere on the display.

Perform additional actions. Some items offer several actions—listen for "actions available" when you select an item. Swipe up or down to choose an action, then double-tap to perform it. (For example, when you select the watch face, you can swipe up or down to choose from go-toglances and go-to-notification-center actions.)

Pause reading. To have VoiceOver stop reading, tap the display with two fingers. Tap again with two fingers to resume.

Adjust VoiceOver volume. Double-tap and hold with two fingers, then slide up or down. Or, open the Apple Watch app on iPhone, tap My Watch, then go to General > Accessibility > VoiceOver and drag the slider.

Adjust reading rate. Open, the Apple Watch app on iPhone, tap My Watch, then go to General > Accessibility > VoiceOver and drag the sliders.

Turn off the display. For privacy, turn on the screen curtain so no one can see what's on Apple Watch while you use VoiceOver. Open the Settings app on Apple Watch, then turn on General > Accessibility > VoiceOver > Screen Curtain.

Turn off VoiceOver. Open the Settings app, go to General > Accessibility > VoiceOver, then tap the VoiceOver button.

"Turn VoiceOver off."

VoiceOver for Setup. VoiceOver can help you set up your Apple Watch—triple-press the Digital Crown during setup.

Set up Apple Watch using VoiceOver

VoiceOver can help you set up Apple Watch and pair it with your iPhone. To highlight a button or other item, swipe left or right on the display with one finger. Tap to activate the highlighted item.

Set up Apple Watch using VoiceOver

1 If Apple Watch isn't on, turn it on by holding down the side button (below the Digital Crown).

2 On Apple Watch, turn on VoiceOver by triple-clicking the Digital Crown.

3 Swipe right or left on the display to choose a language, then double-tap to select it.

4 Swipe right to highlight the Start Pairing button, then double-tap.

5 On iPhone, turn on VoiceOver by going to Settings > General > Accessibility > VoiceOver.

6 To open the Apple Watch app, go to the iPhone Home screen, swipe right to select the Apple Watch app, then double-tap.

7 To get iPhone ready to pair, swipe right to select the Start Pairing button, then double-tap. The "Hold Apple Watch up to the Camera" screen appears.

8 To try automatic pairing, point the iPhone camera at the watch from about 6 inches away. When you hear the pairing confirmation, you can skip to step 14. If you have difficulty, you can try manual pairing, steps 9 through 13.

9 Swipe right to select the Pair Apple Watch Manually button, then double-tap.

10 On Apple Watch, find your Apple Watch ID: swipe right to the Info About Pairing Apple Watch Manually button, then double-tap. Swipe right once to hear the uni☐ue identifier for your Apple Watch—it'll be something like "Apple Watch 52345".

11 On iPhone, select your Apple Watch: swipe right until you hear the same Apple Watch identifier that was just displayed on Apple Watch, then double-tap.

12 To get your pairing code, on Apple Watch, swipe right until you hear the six-digit pairing code.

13 Enter the pairing code from Apple Watch on iPhone using the keyboard.

CHAPTER 7

CUSTOMIZE YOUR WATCH FACE

You can customize the Apple Watch face so it looks the way you want and provides the functions you need.

Choose from a variety of watch face designs, adjust colors, features, and other details, then add it to your collection so you can switch when you need the right timekeeping tools—or whenever you'd like a change.

Change the watch face. With the watch face showing, firmly press the display, then swipe to see the faces in your collection. When you find the face you want, tap it.

Swipe to see other watch faces.

Tap to add features to your watch face.

You can add special functions—sometimes called complications—to your watch face, so you can instantly check things like stock prices or the weather report.

Add features to the watch face. With the watch face showing, firmly press the display, then tap Customize. Swipe to select a feature, then turn the Digital Crown to adjust.

On some faces, you need to tap a feature to select it. When you're finished, press the Digital Crown to save your changes. Tap the face to switch to it.

Press the display and tap Customize.

Turn the Digital Crown to adjust features.

Add a watch face to your collection. Assemble your own collection of custom faces—even different versions of the same design.

With the current watch face showing, firmly press the display, swipe all the way to the right, then tap the New button (+). Swipe up and down to browse designs, then tap the one you want to add. After you add it, you can customize it.

Tap, swipe up or down to browse watch faces, then tap a watch face to add it.

Delete a face from your collection. Don't use a face much anymore? With the current watch face showing, firmly press the display, swipe to the face you don't want, then swipe it up and tap Delete. You can always add the watch face again later.

Swipe up to delete a watch face.

Advance the watch time. Like to set your watch ahead? Open the Settings app, tap Time, tap +0 min, then turn the Digital Crown to set the watch ahead by as much as 59 minutes.

This setting only changes the time shown on the watch face—it doesn't affect alarms, times in notifications, or any other times (such as World Clock).

Turn to advance the time.

Watch faces and features

Apple Watch includes a variety of watch faces, any of which you can customize to suit you. Check fre□uently for software updates; the set of watch faces that follows might differ from what you see on your Apple Watch.

Astronomy

This Astronomy watch face shows you the solar system and the exact position of the planets, sun, and moon, and displays the day, date, and current time.

Tap the Moon to see its current phase.

Tap to see the current position of the planets in the solar system.

While viewing the Earth, moon, or solar system, turn the Digital Crown to move back or forward in time.

Chronograph

This watch face measures time in precise increments, like a classic analog stopwatch. It includes a stopwatch, which can be activated right from the face.

- Adjust basic characteristics: Dial details • Face color
- Add to the watch face: Date • Calendar • Moon phase • Sunrise/Sunset • Weather • Stocks • Activity summary • Alarm • Timer • Battery charge • World Clock

Color

This watch face displays the time and any features you add in your choice of bright colors.

- Adjust basic characteristics: Dial color
- Add to the watch face: Date • Moon phase • Sunrise/sunset • Weather • Activity summary •

Alarm • Timer • Stopwatch • Battery charge • World Clock • Your monogram (displays initials above the center; initials are taken from your Contacts information)

Mickey Mouse

Let Mickey Mouse give you a whimsical view of time, and watch his foot tap off the seconds.

- Add to the watch face: Date • Calendar • Moon phase • Sunrise/sunset • Weather • Activity summary • Alarm • Timer • Stopwatch • Battery charge • World Clock • Expanded views of all the preceding features plus Stocks

Modular

The Modular watch face has a flexible grid design that lets you add many features to give you a thorough view of your day.

• Adjust basic characteristics: Color

• Add to the watch face: Date • Calendar • Moon phase • Sunrise/Sunset • Weather • Stocks •

Activity summary • Alarm • Timer • Stopwatch • Battery charge • World Clock • Expanded views of Calendar, Weather, Stocks, Activity, Alarm, Timer, Stopwatch, and World Clock

Motion

The Motion watch face displays a beautiful animated theme—butterflies, flowers, or jellyfish.

• Adjust basic characteristic: The animated butterfly, flower, or jellyfish

• Add to the watch face: Date (with or without day)

Simple

This minimalistic and elegant watch face lets you add detail to the dial and features to the corners.

• Adjust basic characteristics: Color of the sweep hand • Detail and numbering of the dial

• Add to the watch face: Date • Calendar • Moon phase • Sunrise/Sunset • Weather • Activity summary • Alarm • Timer • Stopwatch • Battery charge • World Clock

Solar

Based on your current location and time of day, the Solar watch face displays the sun's position in the sky, as well as the day, date, and current time.

Turn the Digital Crown to move the sun to dusk, dawn, zenith, sunset, and darkness.

Utility

This watch face is practical and functional; add up to three features to display what you want to see at a glance.

• Adjust basic characteristics: Color of the second hand • Detail and number of the dial

• Add to the watch face: Date • Calendar • Moon phase • Sunrise/Sunset • Weather • Activity summary • Alarm • Timer • Stopwatch • Battery charge • World Clock • Expanded views of all the preceding features plus Stocks

CHAPTER 8

NOTIFICATION AND GLANCES

Respond to unread notifications

See notifications you haven't responded to. If you don't respond to a notification when it arrives, it's saved in Notification Center.

A red dot at the top of your watch face shows you have an unread notification—swipe down to view it. To scroll the notifications list, swipe up or down or turn the Digital Crown.

Swipe down to view unread notifications.

Respond to a notification in the list. Tap the notification.

Tap a notification to respond to it.

Clear notifications. Apple Watch removes notifications from the list when you tap to read them.

To delete a notification without reading it, swipe it to the left, then tap Clear. To clear all notifications, firmly press the display, then tap Clear All.

Tap to clear a notification, or press the display to clear all notifications.

Glances

Get a □uick glance at useful information

From the watch face, you have □uick access to Glances—scannable summaries of the information you view most fre□uently. Swipe up on the watch face to see glances, then swipe left or right to see different glances.

Swipe up on the watch face to see glances.

Check your glances

Swipe up to see glances.

Swipe left or right to view all glances.

Check your glances. Swipe up on the watch face to see the glance you viewed last, then swipe left or right to see other glances. Swipe down to return to the watch face.

When a glance isn't enough. To open the related app, just tap the glance.

Organize your glances

See only what you want to see. To choose your glances, open the Apple Watch app on iPhone, tap My Watch, tap Glances, then remove or include glances. (You can't remove the Settings glance.)

Put them in handy order. Open the Apple Watch app on iPhone, tap My Watch, tap Glances, then drag the reorder buttons.

Drag to change glance order.
Tap to remove a glance.

CHAPTER 9

TIMEKEEPING

To see more information about a city, including time of sunrise and sunset, tap the city in the World Clock list.

When you're finished, tap < in the upper left, or swipe right to return to the city list. As always, you can press the Digital Crown to return to the watch face.

Tap to return to city list.
Press to return to watch face.

Add a city to World Clock. The cities you add on iPhone appear in World Clock on Apple

Watch. Open the Clock app on iPhone, tap World Clock, then tap the Add button (+).

Type a city name or scroll the list.

Add a world clock to your watch face. You can add a world clock to several watch faces—some faces let you add more than one. Firmly press the display, then tap Customize.

Swipe left until you can select individual face features, tap the one you'd like to use for a world clock, then turn the Digital Crown to choose a city.

When you're finished, press the Digital Crown. You can add a world clock to these faces: Chronograph, Color, Mickey Mouse, Modular, Simple, and Utility.

The watch face shows the time in the city you chose.

Turn to the city you want, then press the Digital Crown.

Change city abbreviations.

If you want to change a city abbreviation used on Apple Watch, open the Apple Watch app on iPhone, tap My Watch, then go to Clock > City Abbreviations. Tap any city to change its abbreviation. Change this abbreviation in the Apple Watch app.

Set alarms

Use the Alarm Clock app to play a sound or vibrate Apple Watch at the right time. You can also add an alarm to your watch face, so you can see upcoming alarms at a glance—and open the Alarm Clock app with a tap.

"Set repeating alarm for 6 o'clock PM."

Add an alarm. Open Alarm Clock, firmly press the display, then tap New +. Tap Change Time, tap AM or PM, tap the hours or minutes, and turn the Digital Crown to adjust, then tap Set. Tap < in the upper left to return to the alarm settings, then set repeat, label, and snooze to suit you.

Add alarm. Set alarm time. Select options.

Set or adjust an alarm. Open Alarm Clock, then tap the alarm in the list to change its settings.

Tap next to the alarm to turn it on or off.

Tap to edit alarm.

"Turn off seven-thirty alarm."

See the upcoming alarm on your watch face. With the watch face showing, firmly press the display, then tap Customize.

Swipe left until you can select individual face features, tap the one you'd like to use for alarms, then turn the Digital Crown to choose the alarm.

When you're finished, press the Digital Crown. You can add alarms to these faces: Chronograph, Color, Mickey Mouse, Modular, Simple, and Utility.

View the alarm on your watch face.

Choose an alarm feature to display.

Don't let yourself snooze. When an alarm sounds, you can tap Snooze to wait several minutes before the alarm sounds again. If you don't want to allow snooze, tap the alarm in the list of alarms, then turn off Snooze.

Tap to snooze. Turn off Snooze.

Delete an alarm. Open Alarm Clock, tap the alarm in the list, scroll to the bottom, then tap Delete.

Delete this alarm.

Use a timer

The Timer app on Apple Watch can help you keep track of time. Set timers up to 24 hours.

"Set timer for 20 minutes."

Set a timer. Open Timer, tap hours or minutes, turn the Digital Crown to adjust, then tap Start.

Tap hours or minutes, then turn the Digital Crown.

Set a timer for longer than 12 hours. While adjusting the timer, firmly press the display, then tap 24.

Increase timer length.

Add a timer to your watch face. If you use a timer often, add a timer to your watch face. With the watch face showing, firmly press the display, then tap Customize.

Swipe left until you can select individual face features, tap the one you'd like to use for the timer, then turn the Digital Crown to choose the timer.

When you're finished, press the Digital Crown. You can add a timer to these faces: Chronograph, Color, Mickey Mouse, Modular, Simple, and Utility.

Choose timer feature to display.

View the timer on your watch face.

Scroll to see more options.

Time events with a stopwatch

Time events with accuracy and ease. Apple Watch can time full events (up to 11 hours, 55 minutes) and keep track of lap or split times, then show the results as a list, a graph, or live on your watch face.

The Chronograph watch face has the stopwatch built in, and you can add a stopwatch to these faces: Color, Mickey Mouse, Modular, Simple, and Utility.

Switch to the stopwatch. Open the Stopwatch app, or tap the stopwatch on your watch face (if you've added it or you're using the Chronograph watch face).

Stopwatch controls on the Chronograph watch face

Digital stopwatch

Analog stopwatch

Start, stop, and reset. Tap the Start button. Tap the Lap button to record a lap or split. Tap the Stop button to record the final time.

Timing continues while you switch back to the watch face or open other apps. When you finish, tap the Reset button or the Lap button to reset.

Start or stop the stopwatch.

Record lap times.

Choose the stopwatch format. You can change the format of the timing display before, after, or during timing. Firmly press the display while the stopwatch is showing, then tap Analog, Digital, Graph, or Hybrid.

Switch between analog 1-dial and 3-dial with splits. Swipe up on the 1-dial analog stopwatch display to see separate minute, second, and tenths dials above a scrolling list of lap times.

Review results. Review results on the display you used for timing, or change displays to analyze your lap times and fastest/slowest laps (marked with green and red) in the format you prefer. If the display includes a list of lap times, turn the Digital Crown to scroll.

Slowest lap time

Fastest lap time

Monitor timing from the watch face. To keep an eye on a timing session while displaying your regular watch face, add a stopwatch to the face.

Your current elapsed time will be visible on the face, and you can tap it to switch to the Stopwatch app and check your lap times.

Open Stopwatch app.

Quit using the stopwatch. If you're using the Stopwatch app, just press the Digital Crown. If you're using the Chronograph watch face, the stopwatch controls are always on the face—tap the Lap button to reset.

CHAPTER 10

MESSAGES

Read and reply to messages

You can read incoming text messages right on Apple Watch. You can also reply from Apple Watch, by dictating or choosing a prepared response, or switch to iPhone to type a response.

Read a message. You'll feel a notification tap or hear an alert sound when a message arrives— just raise Apple Watch to read it. Turn the Digital Crown to scroll.

Open a conversation in the Messages app. Tap the Messages icon in the notification.

See a photo in the message. Tap the photo to view it, double-tap it to fill the screen, and drag it to pan.

When you're finished, swipe left from the edge of the photo screen to return to the conversation. If you want to save the photo, open the message in the Messages app on iPhone, and save it there.

Listen to an audio clip in a message. Tap the clip to listen. The clip is deleted after two minutes to save space—if you want to keep it, tap Keep below the clip.

The audio will remain for 30days, and you can set it to remain longer on iPhone: go to Settings > Messages, scroll to Audio Messages, tap Expire, then tap a value.

View a video in a message. In the Messages app, tap a video in a message to start playing the video full-screen. Tap once to display the playback controls.

Double-tap to zoom out and turn the Digital Crown to adjust the volume. Swipe or tap the back button to return to the conversation.

Jump to the top of a long message. In Messages, tap the top of the display.

Reply to a message. If the message just arrived, tap its notification, turn the Digital Crown to scroll to the bottom of the message, then tap Reply.

If it arrived a while ago, swipe down on the watch face to see the message notification, tap it, then scroll to the bottom and tap the Reply button.

To mark the message as read, tap Dismiss or swipe the message. Press the Digital Crown to dismiss the notification without marking the message as read.

Scroll down and tap Reply to respond.

Decide how to be notified. Open the Apple Watch app on iPhone, tap My Watch, then tap Messages. Tap Custom to set options for how you want to be notified when you receive a message.

Set how you want to be notified.

Send and manage messages

Send a new message. Open Messages, firmly press the list of conversations, then tap the New Message icon.

Tap a contact in the list of recent conversations that appears, tap + in the lower left to choose from your full list of contacts, or tap the Microphone button to search for someone in your contacts or to dictate a phone number. There are several ways to compose your message:

• Use preset replies
• Dictate new text
• Record an audio clip
• Send an animated emoji
• Send a map showing your location (if you have your iPhone with you)
• Switch to iPhone and use the full keyboard to type a message

Send a preset reply. When replying to a message, you see a list of handy phrases that you can use—just tap one to send it.

The phrases include contextual responses based on the last message received and six default phrases that you can change. To substitute your own phrases, open the Apple Watch app on iPhone, tap My Watch, go to Messages > Default Replies, then tap a default reply to change it.

If the preset replies aren't in the language you want to use, you can change them by switching to the keyboard for that language in the same conversation in Messages on iPhone.

Cancel your original reply on Apple Watch, then reply again to see the replies in the new language. If you don't want to change keyboards, you can dictate and send an audio clip in the language of your choice.

Dictate or send an animation instead.

Send a preset reply.

Dictate text. While creating a message or reply, tap the Microphone button, say what you want to say, then tap Done.

Don't forget that you can speak punctuation, too (for example, "did it arrive question mark"). You can choose to send the message as a text message or an audio clip—just tap your choice. If you choose audio clip, the recipient gets a voice message to listen to, not a text message to read.

If you use more than one language and your dictation isn't transcribed in the right language for a conversation, you can still send it as an audio clip.

To change the dictation language, change the Siri language on iPhone in Settings > General > Siri, then start a new conversation.

Always send dictated text as an audio clip. If you like to send all your dictated text as an audio clip, you don't need to choose it every time—open the Apple Watch app on iPhone, tap My

Watch, go to Messages > Audio Messages, then tap an option. Include animated emoji. While creating a message or reply, tap the Emoji button, then swipe to browse available images. Turn the Digital Crown to scroll and modify the image (to turn the smile into a frown, for example).

On faces, drag left or right across the eyes or mouth to change the expression further. To see other types of images, swipe to the next pages. The last page lists traditional emoji. When you find the right symbol, tap it to add it to your message, then tap Send.

Scroll to see more variations.

Share your location. To send someone a map showing your current location, firmly press the display while viewing the conversation, then tap Send Location.

Share your location in a message.

Note: On your paired iPhone, make sure Share My Location is turned on in Settings > iCloud >

Share My Location.

See when messages were sent. Swipe left on the conversation in the Messages conversation list.

View message details. Firmly press the display while viewing the conversation, then tap Details to see the contact information of the other participant(s) in the conversation. Or swipe left on the conversation, then tap Details.

Delete a conversation. Swipe left on the conversation, tap Trash, then tap Trash to confirm.

CHAPTER 11

EMAIL

Read mail

Read mail in the Mail app. On Apple Watch, open the Mail app, turn the Digital Crown to scroll the message list, then tap a message. To read the message or reply on iPhone, just swipe up on the Mail icon in the lower-left corner of the iPhone Lock screen.

Swipe up to read mail on iPhone.

Open message to read on

Apple Watch.

Read mail in a notification. If you set Apple Watch to show mail notifications, you can read a new message right in the notification.

Tap the notification when it first appears, or swipe down on the watch face later to see notifications you've received, then tap a mail notification.

To dismiss the notification, swipe down from the top or tap Dismiss at the end of the message.

If you don't receive notifications for mail, go to Settings > Notifications on iPhone and check to see if you have notifications turned on for Mail.

Note: Apple Watch supports most text styles and some formats; ☐uoted text appears in a different color rather than as an indentation. If you receive an HTML message with complex elements, Apple Watch tries to display a text alternative of the message. Try reading the message on your iPhone instead.

Switch to iPhone. Some messages are easier to read in full on iPhone—wake iPhone, then swipe up on the Mail icon in the lower left corner of the lock screen.

Go back to the top of a long mail message. Turn the Digital Crown to scroll ☐uickly, or just tap the top of the display.

Turn to scroll ☐uickly, or tap the top of the display to return to the top of the message.

Open Phone or Maps. Tap a phone number in a mail message to open Phone, or an address to open Maps

See the entire address or subject line. Tap in the To field or the subject line. Apple Watch opens the mail message in its own window, so you can see all the details.

Reply to email. You need to use iPhone to compose a reply—just wake iPhone and swipe up on the mail icon in the lower-left corner of the Lock screen.

Manage mail

Flag a mail message. If you're reading the message in Mail on Apple Watch, firmly press the display, then tap Flag. If you're looking at the message list, swipe left on the message, then tap

More. You can also flag the message when you preview it in a notification—swipe to the Flag button at the bottom of the message. You can unflag a message that's already been flagged.

Note: If you swipe left on a message thread, the action you choose (Flag, Mark as Unread, or Delete) applies to the entire thread.

Change the flag style. Open the Apple Watch app on iPhone, tap My Watch, then go to Mail > Custom > Flag Style.

Mark email as read or unread. If you're reading a message in Mail on Apple Watch, firmly press the display, then tap Unread or Read. If you're looking at the message list, swipe left on the message, then tap More.

Delete email. If you're reading the message in Mail on Apple Watch, firmly press the display, then tap Trash. If you're looking at the message list, swipe left on the message, then tap Trash.

You can also delete a message from its notification—scroll to the bottom of the message, then tap Trash.

Note: If your account is set to archive messages, you'll see an Archive button instead of a Trash button.

Choose which mailbox appears on Apple Watch. Open the Apple Watch app on iPhone, tap My Watch, then go to Mail > Include Mail. You can specify only one mailbox, although if you don't choose a mailbox, you'll see content from all inboxes.

Customize alerts. Open the Apple Watch app on iPhone, tap My Watch, then turn on Mail > Show Alerts. Tap each account or group, turn on the option to be alerted, then choose Sound or Haptic.

If your message list is too long. To make your mail list more compact, you can reduce the number of lines of preview text shown for each email in the list. Open the Apple Watch app on iPhone, tap My Watch, go to Mail > Message Preview, then choose to show 2 lines of the message, 1 line, or none. See 0, 1, or 2 lines of a message.

CHAPTER 12

PHONE CALLS

Answer phone calls

Answer a call. When you feel the incoming call notification, raise your wrist to wake Apple Watch and see who's calling. Tap the Answer button on Apple Watch to talk using the microphone and speaker on Apple Watch.

To scroll to answer the call using iPhone or send a text message instead, turn the Digital Crown to scroll down, then choose an option.

Put the call on hold.

Turn to scroll for more options.

Send a message to the caller.

Send the call to voicemail.

Answer a call.

Hold a call. Tap "Answer on iPhone" to place the call on hold until you can continue it on your paired iPhone.

The caller hears a repeated sound until you pick up the call. If you can't find your iPhone, tap the ping iPhone button on Apple Watch to locate it.

Switch a call from Apple Watch to iPhone. While talking on Apple Watch, just swipe up on the Phone icon in the bottom-left corner of the iPhone Lock screen. Or, if iPhone is unlocked, tap the green bar at the top of the screen.

Adjust call volume. To adjust the speaker volume when talking on Apple Watch, turn the

Digital Crown while on the call or tap the volume symbols on the screen. Tap the Mute button to mute your end of the call (if you're listening on a conference call, for example).

Mute the call.

Adjust volume.

You can also ☐uickly mute an incoming call by pressing the palm of your hand on the watch display and holding it there for three seconds.

You must first turn on the option in the Apple Watch app on iPhone. Go to My Watch > Sounds & Haptics and turn on Cover to Mute.

Send a call to voicemail. Tap the red Decline button in the incoming call notification. Listen to voicemail.

If a caller leaves voicemail, you get a notification—tap the Play button in the notification to listen. To listen to voicemail later, open the Phone app, then tap Voicemail.

Make phone calls

"Call Max."

Place a call. If the person you're calling is one of your favorites, press the side button, turn the Digital Crown or tap their initials, then tap the call button. If they're not in your friends list, open

the Phone app , then tap Favorites or Contacts. Turn the Digital Crown to scroll, then tap the name you want to call.

Call a friend.

See call info on Apple Watch. While you're talking on iPhone, you can view call information on Apple Watch in the Phone app. You can also end the call from Apple Watch (for example, if you're using earphones or a headset).

CHAPTER 13

CALENDARS AND REMINDERS

Check and update your calendar

The Calendar app on Apple Watch shows events you've scheduled or been invited to today and for the next week. Apple Watch shows events for all calendars you use on your iPhone.

Turn to scroll events.

Firmly press to switch between day and list views.

View a monthly calendar.

View your calendar. Open Calendar from the Home screen, or swipe up on the watch face, swipe to the Calendar glance, then tap. You can also tap today's date on your watch face if you've added the calendar to the face.

"What's my next event?"

Review today's events. Open Calendar, then turn the Digital Crown to scroll. Swipe right on today's timeline (Day view) to jump to the current time. To see event details, including time, location, invitee status, and notes, tap the event.

Switch between the daily timeline and a single list of events. Firmly press the display while viewing a daily calendar, then tap List or Day.

View a different day. In Day view, swipe left on today's calendar to see the next day. Swipe right to go back. (You can't see any day before today, or more than seven days total.)

To jump back to the current day and time, firmly press the display, then tap Today. In List view, just turn the

Digital Crown.

See a full month calendar. Tap < in the upper left of any daily calendar. Tap the monthly calendar to return to Day view.

Tap to return to today's events.

Add or modify an event. Switch to the Calendar app on iPhone, then add the event there.

If you're looking at your calendar on Apple Watch, just wake iPhone and swipe up on the Calendar icon in the lower-left corner of the Lock screen to open Calendar.

"Create calendar event titled Gym for May 20 4PM."

Display the date or an upcoming event on the watch face. You can add some combination of day and date to many of the watch faces: for example, Modular, Color, Utility, Simple, or Chronograph.

The Modular, Chronograph, and Mickey Mouse faces can show the next upcoming event. Firmly press the display while viewing the watch face, swipe to a face, then tap Customize.

Respond to an invitation. If you see the invitation when it arrives, just swipe (or turn the Digital Crown to scroll) to the bottom of the notification, then tap Accept, Maybe, or Decline.

If you discover the notification later, tap it in your list of notifications, then scroll and respond. If you're already in the Calendar app, just tap the event to respond.

Swipe up to respond to an invitation.

Contact an event organizer. To email the event organizer, firmly press the display while you're looking at the event details. To send a voice message or call, tap the organizer's name in the event details.

Time to leave. You can schedule a "leave now" alert based on the estimated travel time to an event you create.

Open the Calendar app on iPhone, tap the event, tap Edit, tap Travel Time, and turn it on. You'll get an alert that takes travel time into account.

Get directions to an event.

Adjust settings. Open, the Apple Watch app on iPhone, tap My Watch, then tap Calendar.

Set and respond to reminders

There's no Reminders app on Apple Watch, but Apple Watch notifies you of reminders you create in the Reminders app on your iPhone— and on any other iOS device or Mac that's signed in using your Apple ID. Also, you can create reminders using Siri on Apple Watch.

Respond to a reminder. If you see the reminder notification when it arrives, just swipe (or turn the Digital Crown to scroll) to the bottom of the reminder, then tap Snooze, Completed, or Dismiss. If you discover the notification later, tap it in your list of notifications, then scroll and respond.

Set a reminder. Use Siri on Apple Watch. Press and hold the Digital Crown, then speak. Or just raise your wrist and say "Hey Siri, set a reminder."

You can also set reminders on iPhone or another iOS device or Mac that is signed in using your Apple ID. "Set a reminder for five o'clock."

CHAPTER 14

CHARGING

Charging To charge Apple Watch, use only the Apple Watch Magnetic Charging Cable and included power adapter (and, for Apple Watch Edition, the included Apple Watch Magnetic Charging Case with cable, or the included Apple Watch Magnetic Charging Cable). You may also use third-party Lightning cables and 5W power adapters featuring an MFi logo.

It's important to keep Apple Watch, the Apple Watch Magnetic Charging Cable, and the power adapter in a well-ventilated area when charging.

When charging Apple Watch Edition in the Apple Watch Magnetic Charging Case, keep the case open.

Using a damaged Apple Watch Magnetic Charging Cable or Apple Watch Magnetic Charging Case, or charging when moisture is present, can cause fire, electric shock, injury, or damage to Apple Watch or other property.

Be sure Apple Watch and the Apple Watch Magnetic Charging Cable or Apple Watch

Magnetic Charging Case are dry before charging.

When you use the Apple Watch Magnetic Charging Cable or Apple Watch Magnetic Charging Case to charge Apple Watch, make sure that the USB plug is fully inserted into the adapter before you plug the adapter into a power outlet. Avoid charging Apple Watch in direct sunlight. Don't wear Apple Watch while it is charging.

Lightning cable and connector Avoid prolonged skin contact with the connector when the Lightning to USB Cable is plugged in to a power source because it may cause discomfort or injury. Sleeping or sitting on the Lightning connector should be avoided.

Prolonged heat exposure Apple Watch, the Apple Watch Magnetic Charging Cable, the Apple Watch Magnetic Charging Case, and the power adapter comply with applicable surface temperature standards and limits.

However, even within these limits, sustained contact with warm surfaces for long periods of time may cause discomfort or injury.

Apple Watch, the Apple Watch Magnetic Charging Cable, the Apple Watch Magnetic Charging Case, and the power adapter will become warm when plugged in to a power source.

Use common sense to avoid situations where your skin is in contact with Apple

Watch, the Apple Watch Magnetic Charging Cable, the Apple Watch Magnetic Charging Case, or the power adapter for long periods of time when they're plugged in.

For example, while Apple Watch is charging or while the Apple Watch Magnetic Charging Cable, the Apple Watch Magnetic Charging Case, or the power adapter are plugged in to a power source, don't sleep on them or place them under a blanket, pillow, or your body.

Take special care if you have a physical condition that affects your ability to detect heat against the body. Remove Apple Watch if it becomes uncomfortably warm.

Hearing loss Listening to sound at high volumes may damage your hearing. Background noise, as well as continued exposure to high volume levels, can make sounds seem ☐uieter than they actually are.

Turn on audio playback and check the volume before inserting a Bluetooth connected headset in your ear. For more information about hearing loss, see

CHAPTER 15

HOW TO CLEAN APPLE WATCH

Turn off Apple Watch. Press and hold the side button, then drag the Power Off slider to the right.

Depress the band release buttons and remove the band. See Remove, change, and fasten bands

Wipe Apple Watch clean with a nonabrasive, lint-free cloth. If necessary, you can also lightly dampen the cloth with fresh water.

Dry Apple Watch with a nonabrasive, lint-free cloth.

Apple Watch Edition (gold) models benefit the most if you clean them regularly. Clean with a nonabrasive, lint-free cloth to remove surface oil, perfumes, lotions, and other substances, especially before storing Apple Watch Edition.

The following things are not recommended in the care of your Apple Watch:

Don't clean Apple Watch while it's charging.

Don't dry Apple Watch or the bands using any external heat source (for example, a hair dryer).

Don't use cleaning products or compressed air when cleaning your Apple Watch.

The front of Apple Watch is made of Ion-X glass (strengthened glass) or sapphire crystal, each with a fingerprint-resistant oleophobic (oil repellent) coating. This coating wears over time with normal usage.

Cleaning products and abrasive materials will further diminish the coating, and may scratch the glass or the sapphire crystal.

Using buttons, Digital Crown, connectors, and ports never apply excessive pressure to a button or the Digital Crown on Apple Watch, or force a charging connector into a port, because this may cause damage that is not covered under the warranty.

If the connector and port don't join with reasonable ease, they probably don't match.

Check for obstructions and make sure that the connector matches the port and that you have positioned the connector correctly in relation to the port.

Certain usage patterns can contribute to the fraying or breaking of cables. The cable attached to a charging unit, like any other metal wire or cable, is subject to becoming weak or brittle if repeatedly bent in the same spot.

Aim for gentle curves instead of angles in the cable. Regularly inspect the cable and connector for any kinks, breaks, bends, or other damage. Should you find any such damage, discontinue use of the cable.

Lightning to USB Cable Discoloration of the Lightning connector after regular use is normal. Dirt, debris, and exposure to moisture may cause discoloration.

If your Lightning cable or connector become warm during use or if Apple Watch won't charge or sync, disconnect the cable from the power adapter and clean the Lightning connector with a nonabrasive, dry, lintfree cloth.

Do not use liquids or cleaning products when cleaning the Lightning connector.

Magnetic Charging Cable and Magnetic Charging Case Discoloration of the charging surface of the Apple Watch Magnetic Charging Cable and the Apple Watch Magnetic Charging Case may occur after regular use due to dirt and debris that come in contact with the magnetic surface.

This is normal. Cleaning the magnetic charging surface may reduce, or prevent, such discoloration, and will help to prevent damage to your charger and Apple Watch.

To clean the charging surface, disconnect the charger from both Apple Watch and the power adapter and wipe with a damp, nonabrasive cloth.

Dry with a nonabrasive, lint-free cloth before resuming charging. Do not use cleaning products when cleaning the charging surface.

Operating temperature Apple Watch is designed to work best in ambient temperatures between 32° and 95° F (0° and 35° C) and be stored in temperatures between -4° and 113° F (-20° and 45° C). Apple Watch can be damaged and battery life shortened if stored or operated outside of these temperature ranges.

Avoid exposing Apple Watch to dramatic changes in temperature or humidity. If the interior temperature of Apple Watch exceeds normal operating temperatures (for example, in a hot car or in direct sunlight for extended periods of time), you may experience the following as it attempts to regulate its temperature:

• Charging may slow or stop.

• The display may dim.

• A temperature warning screen may appear.

• Some data transfer may be paused or delayed.

• Some apps may close.

You may not be able to use Apple Watch while the temperature warning screen is displayed. If Apple Watch can't regulate its internal temperature, it goes into Power Reserve or a deep sleep mode until it cools.

Move Apple Watch to a cooler location out of direct sunlight and wait a few minutes before trying to use Apple Watch again.

Magnets Keep key cards and credit cards away from Apple Watch, the bands, the Apple Watch Magnetic Charging Cable, and the Apple Watch Magnetic Charging Case.

Band care information

Use only Apple branded or Apple authorized bands.

How to clean the bands

Remove the band from Apple Watch before cleaning. See Remove, change, and fasten bands, next.

For the leather portions of the bands, wipe them clean with a nonabrasive, lint-free cloth, lightly dampened with fresh water (if necessary).

After cleaning, let the band air dry thoroughly before re-attaching to Apple Watch. Don't store leather bands in direct sunlight, at high temperatures, or in high humidity. Don't soak leather bands in water. The leather bands are not water resistant.

For all other bands and clasps, wipe them clean with a nonabrasive, lint-free cloth, lightly dampened with fresh water (if necessary). Dry the band thoroughly with a nonabrasive, lint-free cloth before re-attaching to Apple Watch.

CHAPTER 16

GET INFORMATION ABOUT YOUR APPLE WATCH

See information about Apple Watch. On Apple Watch, open the Settings app from the Home screen, then go to General > About. The items you can view include:
- Name
- Number of songs, photos, and apps
- Capacity and available storage space
- Software version
- Model number
- Serial number
- Wi-Fi and Bluetooth addresses
- SEID
- Legal Info

To view regulatory marks, open Settings, then go to General > Regulatory.

You can also view this information on the paired iPhone—open the Apple Watch app on iPhone, tap My Watch, then go to General > About. Scroll to the bottom and tap Legal to view Legal Notices, License, information on where to find the Warranty, and RF Exposure information.

Restore Apple Watch

If Apple Watch is disabled because you forgot your passcode or entered an incorrect passcode too many times, you can use the Apple Watch app on iPhone to allow you to enter the passcode again. If you still can't remember your passcode, you can restore Apple Watch and reset the passcode.

Restoring erases the content and settings on Apple Watch, but uses a backup to replace your data and settings. For more information, see Update Apple Watch software, below.

If Erase Data is turned on, the data on your Apple Watch is erased after 10 failed passcode attempts.

CHAPTER 17

USE AND ORGANIZE APPS

Apple Watch includes apps for a variety of communication, information, and timekeeping tasks.

They're on a single Home screen, where you can arrange them as you like. Open an app. From the watch face, press the Digital Crown to get to the Home screen, then tap the app icon. Or turn the Digital Crown to open whichever app is in the center of the Home screen.

Return to the last app. Double-click the Digital Crown.

Return to the watch face. Tap the watch icon on the Home screen to return to your watch face. Or press the Digital Crown.

Rearrange your apps. On Apple Watch, press the Digital Crown to go to the Home screen. Touch and hold an app until the apps jiggle and the app icons look the same size, then drag the app you want to move to a new location. Press the Digital Crown when you're done.

Touch and hold an app, then drag to a new location.

Or open the Apple Watch app on iPhone, tap My Watch, then tap App Layout. Touch and hold an app icon, then drag it to a new location. Tap Reset to restore the original layout.

Touch and drag to move apps around.

Find and install apps from the App Store.

Open the Apple Watch app on iPhone, then tap App Store to find apps for Apple Watch. Purchase, download, and install apps on your iPhone. On Apple Watch, you'll see a message prompting you to install the app. Tap Yes.

See featured Apple Watch apps in the App Store.

Open settings for Apple Watch.

Learn more about Apple Watch.

Adjust settings for installed apps. Open the Apple Watch app on iPhone, tap My Watch, and scroll down to view your apps. Tap an app name to change its settings.

Check storage used by apps. Open the Apple Watch app on iPhone, tap My Watch, then go to General > Usage. View the storage used by each app and the available storage left on Apple Watch.

Hide an installed app from Apple Watch. On the Home screen, touch and hold the app icon until you see an X on the border. Tap the X to remove the app from Apple Watch. It remains installed on your paired iPhone, unless you delete it from there.

To show or hide installed apps on Apple Watch, open the Apple Watch app on iPhone, tap My Watch, scroll down to see apps you've installed, tap the app name, and then tap Show App on Apple Watch.

You can't hide the apps that came with Apple Watch. For information on showing or hiding glances, see Check your glances on page 30.

App icons

Here are the icons for the apps that come with Apple Watch, with links to learn more about them.

• Activity
• Alarm
• Calendar
• Camera
• Mail
• Maps
• Messages
• Music
• Passbook
• Phone
• Photos
• Remote

- Settings
- Stocks
- Stopwatch
- Timer See
- Weather.
- Workout
- World Clock

CHAPTER 18

HOW TO CHOOSE THE BEST APPLE WATCH DOCK?

Apple watch is one of the most recognized and popular smart watch brands in the world. It is known for its amazing features such as the state of the art design and superlative user interface.

Since its inception in the market, these watches have stood apart in its league, as they are well known for utmost customer satisfaction and pride of ownership due to its famous brand name.

Apple watches are □uite expensive and it is essential that the customer invests a decent amount of money on various accessories like docks and stands to safeguard them from damages or misplacing them.

Here are the main factors that need to be considered, listed below:

1. Design: These docks can be designed with a considerably different level of sophistication. They come in various forms and shapes like pucks, rectangular, boxy frames, stands and tubes based on the buyer's re□uirement.

The docks must be designed in such a way that there shouldn't be any damage to the watch from the wristband and the metallic part of the watch getting scuffed up.

Apart from this, they should also be designed to facilitate a stable charging connection when it is mounted on the dock, when not in use. The charging docks should also serve as elegant displays for the watch, as well.

A buyer should be aware of the fact that the more minimalist the design, the easier it is to handle the e□uipment.

2. Quality: The built □uality of the Apple watch charging stands depends on the type of material used in the making of them.

Based on the fixtures involved, the orientation of the stand, parts involved and method of manufacturing; the quality of these docks varies.

The buyer should be aware of the design considerations and the robustness of the materials used before buying them.

3. Cost: These docks cost the buyer anywhere from around $5 up to $150 based on the design, features it has to offer, the materials used to manufacture them and the reliability of the dock.

4. Warranty: Most Apple Watch charging docks have warranties of up to a year or more, so as to insure the dock and the watches from theft or damage.

The buyer should be aware of the warranty and replacement policies before buying the watch dock suitable for their needs.

Thus, in order to buy the best Apple watch dock suitable for the customer's needs, one should consider the aforementioned factors and then proceed to buy the watch dock.

CHAPTER 19

KEEPING A TRACK OF YOUR HEALTH WITH THE NEW APPLE WATCH

The all new Apple Watch has some uni□ue new health and fitness features that help you stay motivated in achieving your fitness levels.

An innovation in the world of wearable technology, this tech watch can monitor your heart rate, measure your steps and calories burnt and keep a track of your workouts.

Whether you are aiming to lose weight and or gain cardio, the Activity, Workout and Health apps in an Apple Watch can help you do all of it.

Check your heart rate

The Apple Watch has a custom heart rate sensor to monitor your heart rate. As long as the user wears the Apple Watch, it will automatically measure and log your heart rate every ten minutes.

All data related to your heart rate will be then sent to the Health app on your iPhone.

It will occur more fre☐uently during your workout sessions, helping you check your intensity level. However, the user can always make adjustments in the settings.

You can always see your heart rate on the Apple Watch in the Heart Rate Glance, where your heart beat is already present by default. In case the user removes it, he will be re☐uired to add it back for him to manually check his heart rate. Simply tap on Glances to add Heartbeat glance again.

View your Activity levels

The Activity app on your Apple Watch will keep a track of the time you spend sitting, moving and exercising. Each of the three activities is represented by three different colored rings - Stand Ring, Move Ring and Exercise Ring.

Here inside the Activity app you will be able to view how far you have reached towards your goal.

The aim obviously is to meet the goals for which you will have to stand for at least a minute each hour for 12 hours, exercise for 30 minutes and achieve your daily calorie goal.

The Activity app basically acts like a visual snapshot of your daily activity, allowing you to check your progress rate whenever you want.

Set a calorie goal activity

To stay fit with the Apple Watch, you will have to set personal goals for yourself. The built-in Activity app on this tech wear allows the user to set calorie burning goals on a daily basis. The user can meet goals by keeping a track of the Activity levels and act accordingly.

You will have to begin from a starting goal. Upon successful completion, the rings of the Activity app will come closer to form a full circle.

Remember the goal is applicable only for active calories and not resting ones. Also the calorie goal can be adjusted anytime but the exercise and stand goals remain static.

Track your workout sessions

With your Apple Watch the user can log all types of workouts right there on his wrist.

Whether you are running on the treadmill or jogging in the park, or going out for a late evening walk with your pet, the Apple Watch on your wrist is going to calculate each and every move of yours.

It will record the entire session and accumulate all details like heart rate, distance, time and others after which it will transfer the data to the Health and Activity apps on your iPhone. For more information please visit Mobile Apps Development Company.

CONCLUSION

The Apple watch at first glance looks much like your typical wristwatch but with many innovative features. It has two different sizes, for people with both small and larger wrists. There are different variations of the Apple watch.

The first is made of stainless steel, the second from luxurious 18-carat gold and third is made of aluminum.

The watch straps are to be available come in a number of colors and materials. The Apple

Watch will also be interchangeable using magnetic technology.

It is important to note that the Apple watch is NOT a stand-alone device. It is connected via Bluetooth and Wi-fi to an iPhone running iOS. It will not work independently and like the Samsung Galaxy Gear, must be connected to an Apple device.

If you are an android user then it's probably not a good idea to by an Apple Watch as you will need to switch to the iOS platform in order for the watch to function.

The screen is made from sapphire crystal glass that has a strong resistance to scrapes and scratches.

Let's face it, there is not point having a $349 watch if it damages easily. It also has a very sensitive touchscreen that can sense the slightest touch or tap.

Its tap function will let you easily select an item on the screen and it also has "force touch" that is the e□uivalent to right clicking on a mouse for faster access.

The Apple watch features a "Digital Crown" which enables you to turn or twist the crown for zooming functions and it can also be pressed.

This is something that Apple is very proud of as the digital crown is a uni□ue and innovative advancement.

The digital crown functions alongside the touchscreen and has a click wheel control. It enables you to zoom in and out and scroll up and down completely eliminating to need for pinch and zoom.

The digital crown also acts as the home but and will return you to the app menu when pressed.

The Apple Watch also has a built-in taptic engine which vibrates on your wrist to alert you when you receive a notification such as an incoming messages or email. It's also integrated through Siri, an intelligent personal assistant and serves as your navigator.

There are a range of apps designed for the Apple Watch. A mini notification system called "Glances" provides for instant notifications. Glances provided a user interface of all relevant notifications from apps such as maps, passbook, photos, messages, weather and mail.

It also has the Friends app which gives you a convenient way to connect with your friends by tapping on your friend's image to send a message or even make a phone call.

You can even send a reply directly through the Apple Watch without having to interact with your iPhone. The Apple Watch comes with integrated audio capabilities including a fully operational speaker and microphone.

The Apple Watch functions as a monitoring device for your health and fitness activities. It holds a number of health and fitness apps that give you a tailored experience in providing health related information such as calorie burn performance.

It also includes a workout app that will display your exercise stats and progress.

The Apple Watch has a number of small sensors to perform functions like tracking your heart beat and the number of steps you take. The new Apple Pay has been integrated into the Apple Watch too.

You will be able to directly pay for purchases by swiping the watch though Apply Pay, Apples new money payment system.

It is far too early to give a definitive answer as to whether the Apple Watch will be a game changer and set the standard to become a must have gadget. It's important to note that this is NOT the first smart watch to be developed but it does have a number of highly competitive features when compared to other smart watch models currently available on the market today.

The simple fact it is an Apple product will also help Apple gain more attention than some of it's lesser known rivals with fewer features.

Another factor to consider that sets the Apple watch apart from the competition is the elegant and premium design that Apple has chosen to develop.

The device may very well turn out to be just a gimmick, but it certainly is a nice one. Other companies like Samsung who have created a smart watch before have so far failed to generate a successful impact on customers. Will Apple be different I wonder?

There does seem to be a fairly substantial amount of initial interest in the Apple Watch both in the media and online.

So maybe this kind of wearable technology is what customers want since it's an entirely new experience and very different from interacting via smartphones or tablets.

Game changer or a gimmick, the Apple Watch is still a great early breakthrough in the wearable technology industry.

There will almost certainly be a number of future updates / improvements by Apple through the coming months to streamline and enrich this product based on feedback.

The Apple Watch still has a great opportunity to set the standard for wearable devices. Even as a gimmick it showcases the best technology design and is an excellent idea in principle.

www.ingramcontent.com/pod-product-compliance
Lightning Source LLC
Chambersburg PA
CBHW071306050326
40690CB00011B/2540